50 Regional Pasta Dishes of Italy

By: Kelly Johnson

Table of Contents

- Spaghetti Carbonara
- Lasagna Bolognese
- Pesto alla Genovese
- Fettuccine Alfredo
- Orecchiette con Cime di Rapa
- Pasta alla Norma
- Tagliatelle al Ragù
- Ravioli di Ricotta e Spinaci
- Penne all'Arrabbiata
- Bucatini all'Amatriciana
- Tortellini in Brodo
- Linguine alle Vongole
- Gnocchi di Patate
- Cannelloni al Forno
- Spaghetti Aglio e Olio
- Farfalle al Salmone
- Ziti al Forno
- Lasagna Verde
- Fregola Sarda con Vongole
- Maltagliati con Fagioli
- Pici Cacio e Pepe
- Trenette al Pesto
- Ravioli di Carne
- Paccheri al Sugo di Pomodoro
- Spaghetti alle Cozze
- Cannelloni di Carne
- Fettuccine ai Funghi
- Pasta alla Puttanesca
- Tagliolini al Tartufo
- Tagliatelle al Limone
- Spaghetti alle Sarde
- Trofie al Pesto
- Anolini in Brodo
- Pasta e Fagioli
- Orecchiette con Salsiccia
- Lasagna di Verdure

- Fettuccine al Pomodoro Fresco
- Caserecce con Ragu di Cinghiale
- Spaghetti al Pomodoro
- Ravioli di Pesce
- Gnocchi di Ricotta
- Spaghetti con Zucchine e Gamberetti
- Pasta con i Broccoli
- Fusilli al Ragu
- Cavatappi al Pesto
- Trofie con Patate e Fagiolini
- Ravioli al Vapore
- Pici con Sugo di Cinghiale
- Linguine al Limone
- Farfalle alla Crema di Gorgonzola

Spaghetti Carbonara

Ingredients:

- 12 oz spaghetti
- 4 oz pancetta or guanciale, diced
- 2 large eggs
- 1 cup grated Pecorino Romano cheese
- 2 cloves garlic, minced
- Freshly cracked black pepper
- Salt (to taste)
- Fresh parsley, chopped (for garnish)

Instructions:

1. **Cook the Spaghetti:**
   - Bring a large pot of salted water to a boil. Add the spaghetti and cook according to package instructions until al dente. Reserve about 1 cup of pasta water before draining the spaghetti.
2. **Prepare the Sauce:**
   - In a large skillet over medium heat, cook the pancetta or guanciale until crispy, about 5-7 minutes. Add the minced garlic and sauté for an additional minute until fragrant. Remove from heat.
3. **Combine Ingredients:**
   - In a bowl, whisk together the eggs and grated Pecorino Romano cheese until smooth. Add a generous amount of black pepper.
   - Quickly add the hot spaghetti to the skillet with the pancetta, tossing to combine. This will help to slightly cool the pasta and prevent the eggs from scrambling.
4. **Finish the Dish:**
   - Remove the skillet from heat and pour the egg and cheese mixture over the spaghetti, tossing quickly to create a creamy sauce. If the sauce is too thick, add reserved pasta water a little at a time until the desired consistency is reached.
5. **Serve:**
   - Divide the pasta among plates, garnishing with additional cheese, black pepper, and chopped parsley. Enjoy immediately!

Lasagna Bolognese

Ingredients:

- **For the Bolognese Sauce:**
    - 2 tbsp olive oil
    - 1 onion, finely chopped
    - 2 cloves garlic, minced
    - 1 carrot, finely chopped
    - 1 celery stalk, finely chopped
    - 1 lb ground beef (or a mix of beef and pork)
    - 1 can (14 oz) crushed tomatoes
    - 1 cup red wine (optional)
    - 1 cup milk
    - Salt and pepper to taste
    - 1 tsp dried oregano
    - Fresh basil leaves, for garnish
- **For the Lasagna:**
    - 9-12 lasagna noodles (no-boil or regular)
    - 2 cups ricotta cheese
    - 1 cup grated Parmesan cheese
    - 2 cups shredded mozzarella cheese

Instructions:

1. **Make the Bolognese Sauce:**
    - In a large pot, heat olive oil over medium heat. Add the onion, garlic, carrot, and celery. Sauté until softened, about 5-7 minutes.
    - Add the ground beef and cook until browned. Drain excess fat if necessary.
    - Stir in the crushed tomatoes, red wine (if using), milk, salt, pepper, and oregano. Bring to a simmer and reduce heat. Cook for at least 30 minutes, stirring occasionally, until the sauce thickens.
2. **Prepare the Lasagna:**
    - Preheat the oven to 375°F (190°C).
    - In a baking dish, spread a thin layer of Bolognese sauce on the bottom. Layer 3-4 lasagna noodles over the sauce.
    - Spread half of the ricotta cheese over the noodles, followed by a third of the mozzarella cheese and a third of the Bolognese sauce. Repeat the layers: noodles, ricotta, mozzarella, and Bolognese sauce. Finish with a final layer of noodles, the remaining Bolognese sauce, and the remaining mozzarella and Parmesan cheese on top.
3. **Bake the Lasagna:**
    - Cover the baking dish with aluminum foil (to prevent sticking, you can spray the foil with cooking spray). Bake for 25 minutes, then remove the foil and bake for an additional 15-20 minutes, until the cheese is bubbly and golden.

4. **Serve:**
    - Let the lasagna rest for about 10 minutes before slicing. Garnish with fresh basil leaves before serving.

Pesto alla Genovese

Ingredients:

- 2 cups fresh basil leaves
- 2-3 cloves garlic
- 1/4 cup pine nuts (or walnuts)
- 1/2 cup grated Parmigiano-Reggiano cheese
- 1/2 cup extra virgin olive oil
- Salt to taste
- Freshly cracked black pepper (optional)
- 12 oz pasta (like trofie or linguine)

Instructions:

1. **Prepare the Pasta:**
   - Cook the pasta in a large pot of salted boiling water according to package instructions until al dente. Reserve some pasta water, then drain the pasta.
2. **Make the Pesto:**
   - In a food processor, combine the basil leaves, garlic, and pine nuts. Pulse until finely chopped.
   - Add the grated Parmigiano-Reggiano cheese and pulse a few more times.
   - With the processor running, slowly drizzle in the olive oil until the mixture is well combined and smooth. If the pesto is too thick, add a little reserved pasta water to reach your desired consistency. Season with salt and pepper to taste.
3. **Combine:**
   - In a large bowl, toss the drained pasta with the pesto, adding reserved pasta water as needed to coat the pasta evenly.
4. **Serve:**
   - Serve immediately, garnished with extra Parmigiano-Reggiano and a drizzle of olive oil if desired.

Fettuccine Alfredo

Ingredients:

- 12 oz fettuccine pasta
- 1/2 cup unsalted butter
- 1 cup heavy cream
- 1-2 cloves garlic, minced (optional)
- 1 1/2 cups grated Parmigiano-Reggiano cheese
- Salt and freshly cracked black pepper to taste
- Chopped parsley (for garnish)

Instructions:

1. **Cook the Pasta:**
   - Cook the fettuccine in a large pot of salted boiling water until al dente. Reserve about 1 cup of pasta water, then drain the pasta.
2. **Prepare the Sauce:**
   - In a large skillet over medium heat, melt the butter. Add the minced garlic (if using) and sauté for 1-2 minutes until fragrant, but not browned.
   - Pour in the heavy cream and simmer for about 5 minutes, stirring frequently.
3. **Add Cheese:**
   - Gradually whisk in the grated Parmigiano-Reggiano cheese until melted and the sauce is creamy. If the sauce is too thick, add a little reserved pasta water to achieve your desired consistency. Season with salt and pepper.
4. **Combine:**
   - Add the drained fettuccine to the sauce, tossing to coat the pasta evenly.
5. **Serve:**
   - Divide the pasta among plates, garnishing with chopped parsley and extra cheese if desired. Enjoy!

Orecchiette con Cime di Rapa

Ingredients:

- 12 oz orecchiette pasta
- 1 bunch cime di rapa (broccoli rabe), trimmed and roughly chopped
- 3-4 cloves garlic, sliced
- 1/4 cup extra virgin olive oil
- 1/2 tsp red pepper flakes (adjust to taste)
- Salt to taste
- Grated Pecorino Romano cheese, for serving

Instructions:

1. **Cook the Pasta:**
   - Bring a large pot of salted water to a boil. Add the orecchiette and cook for about 5 minutes. Then add the cime di rapa to the pot and cook until both the pasta and greens are tender, about 3-4 more minutes. Reserve some pasta water, then drain.
2. **Prepare the Sauce:**
   - In a large skillet over medium heat, heat the olive oil. Add the sliced garlic and red pepper flakes, sautéing until the garlic is golden and fragrant (about 1-2 minutes).
3. **Combine:**
   - Add the drained orecchiette and cime di rapa to the skillet, tossing to combine. If the mixture seems dry, add a splash of reserved pasta water.
4. **Serve:**
   - Divide the pasta among plates and top with grated Pecorino Romano cheese. Enjoy your Orecchiette con Cime di Rapa!

Pasta alla Norma

Ingredients:

- 12 oz pasta (rigatoni or spaghetti)
- 1 large eggplant, diced
- 2 cups crushed tomatoes
- 3-4 cloves garlic, minced
- 1/2 cup grated Ricotta Salata cheese
- 1/4 cup fresh basil leaves
- 1/4 cup extra virgin olive oil
- Salt and freshly cracked black pepper to taste

Instructions:

1. **Prepare the Eggplant:**
   - Salt the diced eggplant and let it sit for 30 minutes to draw out moisture. Rinse and pat dry.
2. **Cook the Pasta:**
   - Cook the pasta in a large pot of salted boiling water until al dente. Reserve some pasta water, then drain.
3. **Make the Sauce:**
   - In a skillet, heat olive oil over medium heat. Add the eggplant and sauté until golden brown.
   - Add minced garlic and cook until fragrant, about 1 minute. Pour in crushed tomatoes, season with salt and pepper, and simmer for 10-15 minutes.
4. **Combine:**
   - Toss the drained pasta with the sauce, adding reserved pasta water if needed. Stir in fresh basil.
5. **Serve:**
   - Serve topped with grated Ricotta Salata cheese.

Tagliatelle al Ragù

Ingredients:

- 12 oz tagliatelle pasta
- 1 lb ground beef and pork mix
- 1 medium onion, finely chopped
- 1 carrot, finely chopped
- 1 celery stalk, finely chopped
- 2 cloves garlic, minced
- 1 cup red wine
- 2 cups crushed tomatoes
- 1/2 cup whole milk
- Olive oil
- Salt and freshly cracked black pepper
- Grated Parmigiano-Reggiano cheese, for serving

Instructions:

1. **Cook the Vegetables:**
   - In a large skillet, heat olive oil over medium heat. Add onion, carrot, and celery; sauté until softened. Add garlic and cook for 1 minute.
2. **Brown the Meat:**
   - Increase the heat and add the ground meat, cooking until browned.
3. **Deglaze:**
   - Pour in the red wine, scraping the bottom of the pan. Let it reduce by half.
4. **Make the Sauce:**
   - Stir in crushed tomatoes and milk, and season with salt and pepper. Simmer on low heat for about 30-40 minutes, stirring occasionally.
5. **Cook the Pasta:**
   - Cook the tagliatelle in salted boiling water until al dente. Drain and combine with the ragù sauce.
6. **Serve:**
   - Serve with grated Parmigiano-Reggiano on top.

Ravioli di Ricotta e Spinaci

Ingredients:

- 1 package (about 16 oz) fresh or frozen ravioli (ricotta and spinach filling)
- 4 tbsp butter
- 1/2 cup fresh sage leaves
- Grated Parmigiano-Reggiano cheese
- Salt and freshly cracked black pepper

Instructions:

1. **Cook the Ravioli:**
   - Boil the ravioli in salted water according to package instructions. Drain, reserving some pasta water.
2. **Make the Sage Butter:**
   - In a skillet, melt butter over medium heat. Add sage leaves and cook until fragrant and the butter begins to brown.
3. **Combine:**
   - Add the drained ravioli to the skillet and toss gently to coat. If the dish is too dry, add reserved pasta water.
4. **Serve:**
   - Serve with grated Parmigiano-Reggiano and black pepper.

Penne all'Arrabbiata

Ingredients:

- 12 oz penne pasta
- 3-4 cloves garlic, sliced
- 1/2 tsp red pepper flakes (adjust to taste)
- 1 can (14 oz) crushed tomatoes
- 1/4 cup fresh parsley, chopped
- Olive oil
- Salt to taste

Instructions:

1. **Cook the Pasta:**
    - Cook the penne in salted boiling water until al dente. Reserve some pasta water, then drain.
2. **Make the Sauce:**
    - In a skillet, heat olive oil over medium heat. Add garlic and red pepper flakes, cooking until fragrant.
    - Pour in crushed tomatoes, season with salt, and simmer for 10 minutes.
3. **Combine:**
    - Toss the drained penne with the sauce, adding reserved pasta water as needed.
4. **Serve:**
    - Serve with chopped parsley and additional olive oil if desired.

Bucatini all'Amatriciana

Ingredients:

- 12 oz bucatini pasta
- 6 oz guanciale (or pancetta), diced
- 1 can (14 oz) crushed tomatoes
- 1/2 cup grated Pecorino Romano cheese
- 1/2 tsp red pepper flakes
- Olive oil
- Salt to taste

Instructions:

1. **Cook the Pasta:**
   - Cook the bucatini in salted boiling water until al dente. Reserve some pasta water, then drain.
2. **Cook the Guanciale:**
   - In a skillet, cook the guanciale in a little olive oil over medium heat until crispy.
3. **Make the Sauce:**
   - Add crushed tomatoes and red pepper flakes. Simmer for 10-15 minutes.
4. **Combine:**
   - Toss the drained bucatini with the sauce, adding reserved pasta water if needed.
5. **Serve:**
   - Serve topped with grated Pecorino Romano cheese.

Tortellini in Brodo

Ingredients:

- 12 oz tortellini (fresh or frozen)
- 4 cups chicken or vegetable broth
- 1/2 cup grated Parmigiano-Reggiano cheese
- Fresh parsley, chopped (for garnish)
- Salt and pepper to taste

Instructions:

1. **Prepare the Broth:**
   - In a large pot, bring the broth to a boil. Season with salt and pepper.
2. **Cook the Tortellini:**
   - Add tortellini to the boiling broth and cook according to package instructions.
3. **Serve:**
   - Ladle the soup into bowls and top with grated Parmigiano-Reggiano and chopped parsley.

Linguine alle Vongole

Ingredients:

- 12 oz linguine pasta
- 2 lbs fresh clams (vongole), cleaned
- 4 cloves garlic, minced
- 1/2 cup dry white wine
- 1/4 cup fresh parsley, chopped
- 1/4 cup extra virgin olive oil
- Salt and pepper to taste

Instructions:

1. **Cook the Pasta:**
   - Cook linguine in salted boiling water until al dente. Reserve some pasta water, then drain.
2. **Cook the Clams:**
   - In a large skillet, heat olive oil over medium heat. Add garlic and sauté until fragrant.
   - Pour in white wine and bring to a simmer. Add clams and cover until they open.
3. **Combine:**
   - Toss the drained linguine with the clams and sauce, adding reserved pasta water as needed.
4. **Serve:**
   - Garnish with chopped parsley and serve immediately.

Gnocchi di Patate

Ingredients:

- 2 lbs potatoes (Russet or Yukon Gold)
- 1 cup all-purpose flour (plus more for dusting)
- 1 egg
- Salt
- Grated Parmigiano-Reggiano cheese, for serving
- Olive oil or butter (optional)

Instructions:

1. **Cook the Potatoes:**
    - Boil potatoes in salted water until tender. Drain and let cool. Peel and mash the potatoes until smooth.
2. **Make the Dough:**
    - In a bowl, mix the mashed potatoes with flour, egg, and salt until a soft dough forms. Do not overwork the dough.
3. **Shape the Gnocchi:**
    - Divide the dough into portions. Roll each portion into a rope and cut into 1-inch pieces. Optionally, use a fork to create ridges.
4. **Cook the Gnocchi:**
    - Bring a large pot of salted water to a boil. Cook gnocchi in batches until they float to the surface. Drain.
5. **Serve:**
    - Toss with olive oil or melted butter, and serve with grated Parmigiano-Reggiano.

Cannelloni al Forno

Ingredients:

- 12-16 cannelloni tubes
- 2 cups ricotta cheese
- 1 cup grated Parmesan cheese
- 1 egg
- 2 cups spinach, cooked and chopped
- 2 cups marinara sauce
- 1 cup mozzarella cheese, shredded
- Salt and pepper to taste
- Fresh basil leaves, for garnish

Instructions:

1. **Prepare the Filling:**
     - In a bowl, mix ricotta, Parmesan, egg, chopped spinach, salt, and pepper.
2. **Stuff the Cannelloni:**
     - Using a piping bag or a spoon, fill each cannelloni tube with the ricotta mixture.
3. **Layer the Dish:**
     - Preheat oven to 375°F (190°C). Spread some marinara sauce on the bottom of a baking dish. Arrange the stuffed cannelloni in a single layer and cover with remaining marinara sauce. Sprinkle mozzarella on top.
4. **Bake:**
     - Cover with aluminum foil and bake for 25 minutes. Remove foil and bake for an additional 15 minutes until cheese is bubbly and golden.
5. **Serve:**
     - Garnish with fresh basil leaves before serving.

Spaghetti Aglio e Olio

Ingredients:

- 12 oz spaghetti
- 4 cloves garlic, thinly sliced
- 1/2 cup extra virgin olive oil
- 1/2 tsp red pepper flakes
- Salt, to taste
- Fresh parsley, chopped, for garnish
- Grated Parmesan cheese, for serving (optional)

Instructions:

1. **Cook the Pasta:**
   - Boil spaghetti in salted water until al dente. Reserve 1 cup of pasta water, then drain.
2. **Make the Sauce:**
   - In a large skillet, heat olive oil over medium heat. Add garlic and red pepper flakes, sautéing until garlic is golden (about 2 minutes).
3. **Combine:**
   - Add the drained spaghetti to the skillet, tossing to coat. If needed, add reserved pasta water to create a silky sauce.
4. **Serve:**
   - Serve with fresh parsley and grated Parmesan cheese.

Farfalle al Salmone

Ingredients:

- 12 oz farfalle pasta
- 8 oz smoked salmon, cut into strips
- 1 cup heavy cream
- 1/2 cup white wine
- 1 shallot, finely chopped
- 2 tbsp capers
- 1 tbsp lemon juice
- Olive oil
- Fresh dill, for garnish
- Salt and pepper to taste

Instructions:

1. **Cook the Pasta:**
   - Boil farfalle in salted water until al dente. Reserve some pasta water, then drain.
2. **Make the Sauce:**
   - In a skillet, heat olive oil and sauté shallot until translucent. Add white wine and reduce by half. Stir in heavy cream, capers, and lemon juice.
3. **Combine:**
   - Add smoked salmon and cooked farfalle to the sauce. Toss gently, adding reserved pasta water if needed.
4. **Serve:**
   - Garnish with fresh dill before serving.

Ziti al Forno

Ingredients:

- 12 oz ziti pasta
- 1 lb ground beef or sausage
- 2 cups marinara sauce
- 1 cup ricotta cheese
- 2 cups mozzarella cheese, shredded
- 1/2 cup grated Parmesan cheese
- 1 egg
- Salt and pepper to taste
- Fresh basil, for garnish

Instructions:

1. **Cook the Pasta:**
    - Boil ziti in salted water until al dente. Drain and set aside.
2. **Make the Meat Sauce:**
    - In a skillet, brown the ground meat. Stir in marinara sauce and let simmer for 10 minutes.
3. **Prepare the Cheese Mixture:**
    - In a bowl, mix ricotta, egg, salt, and pepper.
4. **Layer the Dish:**
    - Preheat oven to 375°F (190°C). In a baking dish, layer half of the cooked ziti, followed by half of the meat sauce, dollops of the ricotta mixture, and half of the mozzarella. Repeat layers and top with remaining mozzarella and Parmesan.
5. **Bake:**
    - Bake for 25-30 minutes until the top is bubbly and golden.
6. **Serve:**
    - Garnish with fresh basil before serving.

Lasagna Verde

Ingredients:

- 9 lasagna noodles
- 2 cups spinach, cooked and chopped
- 1 cup ricotta cheese
- 1 cup grated Parmesan cheese
- 2 cups marinara sauce
- 2 cups mozzarella cheese, shredded
- 1 egg
- Salt and pepper to taste
- Fresh basil leaves, for garnish

Instructions:

1. **Cook the Noodles:**
   - Boil lasagna noodles until al dente. Drain and set aside.
2. **Prepare the Filling:**
   - In a bowl, mix spinach, ricotta, egg, salt, and pepper.
3. **Layer the Dish:**
   - Preheat oven to 375°F (190°C). In a baking dish, spread some marinara sauce on the bottom. Layer noodles, spinach filling, marinara sauce, and mozzarella. Repeat until all ingredients are used.
4. **Bake:**
   - Cover with aluminum foil and bake for 30 minutes. Remove foil and bake for an additional 15 minutes until cheese is golden.
5. **Serve:**
   - Garnish with fresh basil before serving.

Fregola Sarda con Vongole

Ingredients:

- 1 cup fregola sarda
- 2 lbs fresh clams (vongole), cleaned
- 4 cloves garlic, minced
- 1/2 cup dry white wine
- 2 cups vegetable broth
- 1/4 cup fresh parsley, chopped
- Olive oil
- Salt and pepper to taste

Instructions:

1. **Cook the Fregola:**
   - In a pot, heat olive oil and add garlic. Sauté until fragrant. Add fregola and toast for a few minutes.
2. **Add Clams and Broth:**
   - Pour in white wine and let it evaporate. Add clams and vegetable broth, covering the pot until clams open.
3. **Combine:**
   - Once clams are open, mix everything together, adding parsley and seasoning with salt and pepper.
4. **Serve:**
   - Serve warm, garnished with extra parsley.

Maltagliati con Fagioli

Ingredients:

- 1 cup maltagliati pasta (or any irregular pasta)
- 1 can (15 oz) cannellini beans, drained and rinsed
- 4 cups vegetable broth
- 2 cloves garlic, minced
- 1 small onion, chopped
- 1 carrot, diced
- 1 celery stalk, diced
- Olive oil
- Fresh parsley, for garnish
- Salt and pepper to taste

Instructions:

1. **Cook the Vegetables:**
   - In a pot, heat olive oil and sauté onion, carrot, and celery until softened. Add garlic and cook for 1 minute.
2. **Add Broth and Beans:**
   - Pour in vegetable broth and bring to a boil. Stir in cannellini beans and let simmer for 10 minutes.
3. **Cook the Pasta:**
   - Add maltagliati to the pot and cook until al dente.
4. **Serve:**
   - Season with salt and pepper, and garnish with fresh parsley.

Pici Cacio e Pepe

Ingredients:

- 12 oz pici pasta (or spaghetti)
- 1 cup grated Pecorino Romano cheese
- 1 tsp freshly cracked black pepper
- Salt, to taste
- Olive oil (optional)

Instructions:

1. **Cook the Pasta:**
    - Boil pici in salted water until al dente. Reserve some pasta water, then drain.
2. **Make the Sauce:**
    - In a large bowl, combine Pecorino Romano cheese and cracked black pepper.
3. **Combine:**
    - Add the hot pasta to the cheese mixture, tossing to coat. If needed, add reserved pasta water to create a creamy sauce.
4. **Serve:**
    - Serve immediately with extra cheese and black pepper on top.

Trenette al Pesto

Ingredients:

- 12 oz trenette pasta (or linguine)
- 2 cups fresh basil leaves
- 1/2 cup extra virgin olive oil
- 1/4 cup pine nuts
- 1/2 cup grated Parmigiano-Reggiano cheese
- 2 cloves garlic
- Salt, to taste
- 1/4 cup water (as needed)

Instructions:

1. **Cook the Pasta:**
   - Boil trenette in salted water until al dente. Reserve some pasta water, then drain.
2. **Make the Pesto:**
   - In a food processor, combine basil, pine nuts, garlic, and a pinch of salt. Pulse until finely chopped. With the processor running, slowly add olive oil until a smooth paste forms. Stir in Parmigiano-Reggiano.
3. **Combine:**
   - In a large bowl, toss the cooked pasta with pesto, adding reserved pasta water as needed for desired consistency.
4. **Serve:**
   - Serve immediately, garnished with extra cheese and pine nuts.

Ravioli di Carne

Ingredients:

- 1 package fresh or frozen meat ravioli (about 16 oz)
- 2 cups marinara sauce
- 1/2 cup grated Parmigiano-Reggiano cheese
- 1/4 cup fresh parsley, chopped
- Salt and pepper to taste

Instructions:

1. **Cook the Ravioli:**
    - Boil ravioli in salted water according to package instructions until they float to the surface. Drain and set aside.
2. **Heat the Sauce:**
    - In a saucepan, warm marinara sauce over medium heat.
3. **Combine:**
    - Gently toss the cooked ravioli in the marinara sauce. Season with salt and pepper.
4. **Serve:**
    - Serve garnished with grated cheese and fresh parsley.

Paccheri al Sugo di Pomodoro

Ingredients:

- 12 oz paccheri pasta
- 4 cups crushed tomatoes (canned or fresh)
- 2 cloves garlic, minced
- 1/4 cup olive oil
- 1/4 cup fresh basil leaves
- Salt and pepper to taste
- Grated Parmigiano-Reggiano cheese, for serving

Instructions:

1. **Cook the Pasta:**
   - Boil paccheri in salted water until al dente. Drain and set aside.
2. **Make the Sauce:**
   - In a skillet, heat olive oil and sauté garlic until fragrant. Add crushed tomatoes and simmer for about 15 minutes. Season with salt and pepper.
3. **Combine:**
   - Toss cooked paccheri in the tomato sauce and mix well. Add fresh basil.
4. **Serve:**
   - Serve hot, garnished with grated cheese.

Spaghetti alle Cozze

Ingredients:

- 12 oz spaghetti
- 2 lbs fresh mussels, cleaned
- 4 cloves garlic, minced
- 1/2 cup white wine
- 1/4 cup olive oil
- 1/4 tsp red pepper flakes
- Fresh parsley, chopped, for garnish
- Salt and pepper to taste

Instructions:

1. **Cook the Pasta:**
    - Boil spaghetti in salted water until al dente. Reserve some pasta water, then drain.
2. **Prepare the Mussels:**
    - In a large pot, heat olive oil and sauté garlic and red pepper flakes. Add mussels and white wine, covering until mussels open (about 5-7 minutes).
3. **Combine:**
    - Add the drained spaghetti to the pot with mussels, tossing gently. Add reserved pasta water if needed.
4. **Serve:**
    - Garnish with fresh parsley and serve immediately.

Cannelloni di Carne

Ingredients:

- 12-16 cannelloni tubes
- 1 lb ground beef or sausage
- 1 cup ricotta cheese
- 1 cup marinara sauce
- 1/2 cup grated Parmigiano-Reggiano cheese
- 1 egg
- 1/4 cup fresh parsley, chopped
- Salt and pepper to taste

Instructions:

1. **Prepare the Filling:**
    - In a skillet, brown the meat. In a bowl, mix cooked meat, ricotta, egg, parsley, salt, and pepper.
2. **Stuff the Cannelloni:**
    - Fill each cannelloni tube with the meat mixture.
3. **Layer the Dish:**
    - Preheat oven to 375°F (190°C). Spread some marinara sauce on the bottom of a baking dish. Arrange stuffed cannelloni in the dish, top with remaining sauce and sprinkle with Parmigiano-Reggiano.
4. **Bake:**
    - Cover with foil and bake for 25-30 minutes. Remove foil and bake for an additional 10 minutes.
5. **Serve:**
    - Garnish with fresh herbs before serving.

Fettuccine ai Funghi

Ingredients:

- 12 oz fettuccine pasta
- 8 oz mixed mushrooms, sliced
- 4 cloves garlic, minced
- 1 cup heavy cream
- 1/2 cup grated Parmigiano-Reggiano cheese
- 2 tbsp olive oil
- Salt and pepper to taste
- Fresh parsley, chopped, for garnish

Instructions:

1. **Cook the Pasta:**
    - Boil fettuccine in salted water until al dente. Reserve some pasta water, then drain.
2. **Prepare the Mushrooms:**
    - In a skillet, heat olive oil and sauté garlic until fragrant. Add mushrooms and cook until browned.
3. **Make the Sauce:**
    - Stir in heavy cream and bring to a simmer. Add cooked fettuccine and toss, adding reserved pasta water for desired consistency.
4. **Serve:**
    - Serve hot, garnished with grated cheese and fresh parsley.

Pasta alla Puttanesca

Ingredients:

- 12 oz spaghetti or linguine
- 3 tbsp olive oil
- 4 cloves garlic, minced
- 1/2 tsp red pepper flakes
- 1 can (14 oz) diced tomatoes
- 1/2 cup black olives, pitted and sliced
- 2 tbsp capers, rinsed
- Fresh parsley, chopped, for garnish
- Salt and pepper to taste

Instructions:

1. **Cook the Pasta:**
    - Boil pasta in salted water until al dente. Reserve some pasta water, then drain.
2. **Make the Sauce:**
    - In a skillet, heat olive oil and sauté garlic and red pepper flakes. Add diced tomatoes, olives, and capers, simmering for about 10 minutes.
3. **Combine:**
    - Toss cooked pasta in the sauce, adding reserved pasta water if needed.
4. **Serve:**
    - Garnish with fresh parsley before serving.

Tagliolini al Tartufo

Ingredients:

- 12 oz tagliolini pasta
- 1/2 cup heavy cream
- 1/4 cup grated Parmigiano-Reggiano cheese
- 2 tbsp truffle oil
- Salt and pepper to taste
- Fresh truffle shavings (optional, for garnish)

Instructions:

1. **Cook the Pasta:**
    - Boil tagliolini in salted water until al dente. Reserve some pasta water, then drain.
2. **Make the Sauce:**
    - In a skillet, heat heavy cream over medium heat, stirring in truffle oil and cheese. Season with salt and pepper.
3. **Combine:**
    - Add cooked tagliolini to the sauce, tossing gently and adding reserved pasta water if needed.
4. **Serve:**
    - Serve immediately, garnished with truffle shavings if desired.

Tagliatelle al Limone

Ingredients:

- 12 oz tagliatelle pasta
- 1/2 cup heavy cream
- 1/2 cup grated Parmigiano-Reggiano cheese
- Zest of 2 lemons
- Juice of 1 lemon
- 2 tbsp olive oil
- Salt and pepper to taste
- Fresh basil or parsley, for garnish

Instructions:

1. **Cook the Pasta:**
    - Boil tagliatelle in salted water until al dente. Reserve some pasta water, then drain.
2. **Make the Sauce:**
    - In a skillet, heat olive oil and add heavy cream, lemon zest, and lemon juice. Stir and simmer for a few minutes.
3. **Combine:**
    - Toss the cooked pasta in the lemon sauce, adding reserved pasta water as needed. Mix in the grated cheese and season with salt and pepper.
4. **Serve:**
    - Serve garnished with fresh herbs and additional cheese if desired.

Spaghetti alle Sarde

Ingredients:

- 12 oz spaghetti
- 1 can (about 4 oz) sardines in oil, drained
- 2 tbsp olive oil
- 1 onion, finely chopped
- 2 cloves garlic, minced
- 1/4 cup raisins
- 1/4 cup pine nuts
- 1/2 tsp red pepper flakes
- Salt and pepper to taste
- Fresh parsley, chopped, for garnish

Instructions:

1. **Cook the Pasta:**
    - Boil spaghetti in salted water until al dente. Reserve some pasta water, then drain.
2. **Prepare the Sauce:**
    - In a skillet, heat olive oil and sauté onion and garlic until soft. Add sardines, breaking them up gently.
3. **Combine:**
    - Add raisins, pine nuts, and red pepper flakes. Toss in the cooked spaghetti, adding reserved pasta water as needed to create a sauce. Season with salt and pepper.
4. **Serve:**
    - Garnish with fresh parsley before serving.

Trofie al Pesto

Ingredients:

- 12 oz trofie pasta (or other short pasta)
- 2 cups fresh basil leaves
- 1/2 cup extra virgin olive oil
- 1/4 cup pine nuts
- 1/2 cup grated Parmigiano-Reggiano cheese
- 2 cloves garlic
- Salt, to taste

Instructions:

1. **Cook the Pasta:**
   - Boil trofie in salted water until al dente. Reserve some pasta water, then drain.
2. **Make the Pesto:**
   - In a food processor, combine basil, pine nuts, garlic, and salt. Pulse until finely chopped. With the processor running, add olive oil until smooth. Stir in Parmigiano-Reggiano.
3. **Combine:**
   - Toss the cooked pasta with pesto, adding reserved pasta water for desired consistency.
4. **Serve:**
   - Serve immediately, garnished with additional cheese.

Anolini in Brodo

Ingredients:

- 12 oz anolini pasta (or tortellini)
- 6 cups beef or chicken broth
- 1 cup grated Parmigiano-Reggiano cheese
- Fresh herbs (such as parsley or thyme), for garnish
- Salt and pepper to taste

Instructions:

1. **Prepare the Broth:**
   - In a large pot, heat the broth until simmering. Season with salt and pepper.
2. **Cook the Anolini:**
   - Add anolini to the simmering broth and cook according to package instructions until tender.
3. **Serve:**
   - Ladle the broth and anolini into bowls. Garnish with grated cheese and fresh herbs.

Pasta e Fagioli

Ingredients:

- 8 oz ditalini or small pasta
- 1 can (15 oz) cannellini beans, drained and rinsed
- 4 cups vegetable or chicken broth
- 1 onion, chopped
- 2 cloves garlic, minced
- 1 carrot, diced
- 2 stalks celery, diced
- 1 can (14 oz) diced tomatoes
- 2 tbsp olive oil
- Salt and pepper to taste
- Fresh parsley, chopped, for garnish

Instructions:

1. **Sauté the Vegetables:**
    - In a pot, heat olive oil and sauté onion, garlic, carrot, and celery until softened.
2. **Add Ingredients:**
    - Stir in diced tomatoes, broth, and beans. Bring to a boil, then simmer for about 10 minutes.
3. **Cook the Pasta:**
    - Add pasta and cook until al dente, about 10 minutes. Season with salt and pepper.
4. **Serve:**
    - Serve hot, garnished with fresh parsley.

Orecchiette con Salsiccia

Ingredients:

- 12 oz orecchiette pasta
- 1 lb Italian sausage, removed from casings
- 2 cups broccoli rabe, chopped
- 4 cloves garlic, minced
- 1/4 cup olive oil
- 1/2 tsp red pepper flakes
- Salt and pepper to taste
- Grated Parmigiano-Reggiano cheese, for serving

Instructions:

1. **Cook the Pasta:**
   - Boil orecchiette in salted water until al dente. Add broccoli rabe during the last 3 minutes of cooking. Drain and set aside.
2. **Cook the Sausage:**
   - In a skillet, heat olive oil and sauté garlic and red pepper flakes. Add sausage and cook until browned.
3. **Combine:**
   - Toss the cooked pasta and broccoli rabe in the skillet with the sausage. Season with salt and pepper.
4. **Serve:**
   - Serve hot, garnished with grated cheese.

Lasagna di Verdure

Ingredients:

- 9 lasagna noodles
- 2 cups ricotta cheese
- 2 cups marinara sauce
- 2 cups mixed vegetables (such as spinach, zucchini, and bell peppers), sautéed
- 2 cups grated mozzarella cheese
- 1/2 cup grated Parmigiano-Reggiano cheese
- 1 egg
- Salt and pepper to taste

Instructions:

1. **Cook the Noodles:**
   - Cook lasagna noodles according to package instructions. Drain and set aside.
2. **Prepare the Filling:**
   - In a bowl, mix ricotta, sautéed vegetables, egg, salt, and pepper.
3. **Layer the Lasagna:**
   - Preheat oven to 375°F (190°C). In a baking dish, spread some marinara sauce. Layer with noodles, ricotta mixture, mozzarella, and more sauce. Repeat layers, finishing with sauce and remaining mozzarella and Parmigiano-Reggiano on top.
4. **Bake:**
   - Cover with foil and bake for 30 minutes. Remove foil and bake for an additional 15 minutes.
5. **Serve:**
   - Let cool slightly before slicing and serving.

Fettuccine al Pomodoro Fresco

Ingredients:

- 12 oz fettuccine pasta
- 4 large ripe tomatoes, chopped
- 2 cloves garlic, minced
- 1/4 cup olive oil
- Fresh basil leaves, for garnish
- Salt and pepper to taste
- Grated Parmigiano-Reggiano cheese, for serving

Instructions:

1. **Cook the Pasta:**
    - Boil fettuccine in salted water until al dente. Reserve some pasta water, then drain.
2. **Make the Sauce:**
    - In a skillet, heat olive oil and sauté garlic until fragrant. Add chopped tomatoes and cook until softened. Season with salt and pepper.
3. **Combine:**
    - Toss cooked fettuccine in the sauce, adding reserved pasta water as needed.
4. **Serve:**
    - Serve garnished with fresh basil and grated cheese.

Caserecce con Ragu di Cinghiale

Ingredients:

- 12 oz caserecce pasta
- 1 lb wild boar meat, finely chopped
- 1 onion, chopped
- 2 cloves garlic, minced
- 1 carrot, diced
- 1 celery stalk, diced
- 1 cup red wine
- 1 can (14 oz) diced tomatoes
- 1/4 cup olive oil
- Fresh rosemary, thyme, and bay leaf
- Salt and pepper to taste
- Grated Parmigiano-Reggiano cheese, for serving

Instructions:

1. **Cook the Meat:**
   - In a large pot, heat olive oil over medium heat. Add onion, garlic, carrot, and celery, and sauté until soft. Add wild boar and cook until browned.
2. **Add Wine and Tomatoes:**
   - Pour in red wine, scraping the bottom of the pot. Cook until wine reduces. Add diced tomatoes, herbs, salt, and pepper. Simmer for at least 1 hour.
3. **Cook the Pasta:**
   - Boil caserecce in salted water until al dente. Drain and reserve some pasta water.
4. **Combine:**
   - Toss cooked pasta with the ragu, adding reserved pasta water as needed.
5. **Serve:**
   - Serve hot, garnished with grated cheese.

Spaghetti al Pomodoro

Ingredients:

- 12 oz spaghetti
- 4 large ripe tomatoes, diced
- 2 cloves garlic, minced
- 1/4 cup olive oil
- Fresh basil leaves
- Salt and pepper to taste
- Grated Parmigiano-Reggiano cheese, for serving

Instructions:

1. **Cook the Pasta:**
    - Boil spaghetti in salted water until al dente. Reserve some pasta water, then drain.
2. **Make the Sauce:**
    - In a skillet, heat olive oil and sauté garlic until fragrant. Add diced tomatoes, salt, and pepper. Cook until the tomatoes break down.
3. **Combine:**
    - Toss the cooked spaghetti in the sauce, adding reserved pasta water for desired consistency. Stir in fresh basil.
4. **Serve:**
    - Serve hot, garnished with grated cheese.

Ravioli di Pesce

Ingredients:

- 12 oz fish ravioli (store-bought or homemade)
- 1 cup seafood stock
- 1/2 cup heavy cream
- 1/4 cup white wine
- 2 tbsp olive oil
- 1 clove garlic, minced
- Fresh parsley, chopped, for garnish
- Salt and pepper to taste

Instructions:

1. **Cook the Ravioli:**
    - Boil ravioli in salted water according to package instructions. Drain and set aside.
2. **Prepare the Sauce:**
    - In a skillet, heat olive oil and sauté garlic until fragrant. Add white wine and cook until reduced. Stir in seafood stock and cream, simmering until slightly thickened.
3. **Combine:**
    - Toss the cooked ravioli in the sauce, seasoning with salt and pepper.
4. **Serve:**
    - Serve hot, garnished with fresh parsley.

Gnocchi di Ricotta

Ingredients:

- 1 cup ricotta cheese
- 1 cup all-purpose flour (plus extra for dusting)
- 1 egg
- 1/2 cup grated Parmigiano-Reggiano cheese
- Salt and nutmeg, to taste
- Butter and sage leaves for serving

Instructions:

1. **Make the Dough:**
    - In a bowl, combine ricotta, flour, egg, cheese, salt, and nutmeg. Mix until a soft dough forms.
2. **Shape the Gnocchi:**
    - On a floured surface, roll small pieces of dough into ropes, then cut into small pieces. Press with a fork to shape.
3. **Cook the Gnocchi:**
    - Boil gnocchi in salted water until they float to the surface. Drain.
4. **Serve:**
    - In a skillet, melt butter and add sage leaves. Toss gnocchi in the sage butter and serve hot.

Spaghetti con Zucchine e Gamberetti

Ingredients:

- 12 oz spaghetti
- 1 lb shrimp, peeled and deveined
- 2 zucchinis, sliced
- 2 cloves garlic, minced
- 1/4 cup olive oil
- 1/2 tsp red pepper flakes
- Salt and pepper to taste
- Fresh parsley, for garnish

Instructions:

1. **Cook the Pasta:**
    - Boil spaghetti in salted water until al dente. Reserve some pasta water, then drain.
2. **Sauté the Zucchini and Shrimp:**
    - In a skillet, heat olive oil and sauté garlic and red pepper flakes. Add zucchini and cook until tender. Add shrimp and cook until pink.
3. **Combine:**
    - Toss the cooked spaghetti with the zucchini and shrimp, adding reserved pasta water as needed. Season with salt and pepper.
4. **Serve:**
    - Serve hot, garnished with fresh parsley.

Pasta con i Broccoli

Ingredients:

- 12 oz pasta (such as penne or orecchiette)
- 2 cups broccoli florets
- 2 cloves garlic, minced
- 1/4 cup olive oil
- 1/2 tsp red pepper flakes
- Grated Parmigiano-Reggiano cheese, for serving
- Salt and pepper to taste

Instructions:

1. **Cook the Pasta and Broccoli:**
   - Boil pasta in salted water. Add broccoli florets during the last 3 minutes of cooking. Drain and reserve some pasta water.
2. **Prepare the Sauce:**
   - In a skillet, heat olive oil and sauté garlic and red pepper flakes. Add the cooked pasta and broccoli.
3. **Combine:**
   - Toss everything together, adding reserved pasta water for desired consistency. Season with salt and pepper.
4. **Serve:**
   - Serve hot, garnished with grated cheese.

Fusilli al Ragu

Ingredients:

- 12 oz fusilli pasta
- 1 lb ground beef or pork
- 1 onion, chopped
- 2 cloves garlic, minced
- 1 carrot, diced
- 1 celery stalk, diced
- 1 can (14 oz) crushed tomatoes
- 1/2 cup red wine
- 1/4 cup olive oil
- Fresh basil, for garnish
- Salt and pepper to taste

Instructions:

1. **Cook the Meat:**
    - In a large pot, heat olive oil. Add onion, garlic, carrot, and celery, sautéing until soft. Add meat and cook until browned.
2. **Add Wine and Tomatoes:**
    - Pour in red wine and cook until reduced. Add crushed tomatoes, salt, and pepper, and simmer for about 30 minutes.
3. **Cook the Pasta:**
    - Boil fusilli in salted water until al dente. Drain.
4. **Combine:**
    - Toss the cooked fusilli with the ragu sauce.
5. **Serve:**
    - Serve hot, garnished with fresh basil.

Cavatappi al Pesto

Ingredients:

- 12 oz cavatappi pasta
- 2 cups fresh basil leaves
- 1/2 cup olive oil
- 1/4 cup pine nuts
- 1/2 cup grated Parmigiano-Reggiano cheese
- 2 cloves garlic
- Salt, to taste

Instructions:

1. **Cook the Pasta:**
    - Boil cavatappi in salted water until al dente. Reserve some pasta water, then drain.
2. **Make the Pesto:**
    - In a food processor, combine basil, pine nuts, garlic, and salt. Pulse until finely chopped. With the processor running, add olive oil until smooth. Stir in Parmigiano-Reggiano.
3. **Combine:**
    - Toss the cooked pasta with pesto, adding reserved pasta water for desired consistency.
4. **Serve:**
    - Serve immediately, garnished with additional cheese.

Trofie con Patate e Fagiolini

Ingredients:

- 12 oz trofie pasta
- 2 medium potatoes, peeled and diced
- 2 cups green beans, trimmed
- 1/4 cup olive oil
- 2 cloves garlic, minced
- Salt and pepper to taste
- Grated Parmigiano-Reggiano cheese, for serving

Instructions:

1. **Cook the Vegetables:**
    - In a large pot, bring salted water to a boil. Add diced potatoes and cook for about 5 minutes. Add green beans and cook for an additional 5 minutes.
2. **Cook the Pasta:**
    - Add trofie to the pot and cook until al dente. Reserve some pasta water, then drain the mixture.
3. **Prepare the Sauce:**
    - In a skillet, heat olive oil and sauté minced garlic until fragrant.
4. **Combine:**
    - Toss the cooked pasta and vegetables in the skillet with the garlic oil, adding reserved pasta water as needed. Season with salt and pepper.
5. **Serve:**
    - Serve hot, garnished with grated cheese.

Ravioli al Vapore

Ingredients:

- 12 oz fresh ravioli (your choice of filling)
- 1/4 cup olive oil
- 1/4 cup grated Parmigiano-Reggiano cheese
- Fresh basil, for garnish
- Salt and pepper to taste

Instructions:

1. **Prepare the Steamer:**
   - Fill a pot with water and bring it to a boil. Set a steaming basket over the pot.
2. **Steam the Ravioli:**
   - Place ravioli in the steaming basket in a single layer. Cover and steam for about 5-7 minutes, or until cooked through.
3. **Serve:**
   - Transfer ravioli to a serving plate. Drizzle with olive oil and sprinkle with cheese, salt, and pepper. Garnish with fresh basil.

Pici con Sugo di Cinghiale

Ingredients:

- 12 oz pici pasta
- 1 lb wild boar meat, finely chopped
- 1 onion, chopped
- 2 cloves garlic, minced
- 1 carrot, diced
- 1/2 cup red wine
- 1 can (14 oz) diced tomatoes
- 1/4 cup olive oil
- Fresh rosemary, thyme, and bay leaf
- Salt and pepper to taste

Instructions:

1. **Cook the Meat:**
   - In a large pot, heat olive oil over medium heat. Add onion, garlic, carrot, and sauté until soft. Add wild boar and cook until browned.
2. **Add Wine and Tomatoes:**
   - Pour in red wine and cook until it reduces. Add diced tomatoes, herbs, salt, and pepper. Simmer for at least 1 hour.
3. **Cook the Pici:**
   - Boil pici in salted water until al dente. Drain and reserve some pasta water.
4. **Combine:**
   - Toss the cooked pici with the ragu, adding reserved pasta water as needed.
5. **Serve:**
   - Serve hot, garnished with grated cheese.

Linguine al Limone

Ingredients:

- 12 oz linguine
- 1/4 cup olive oil
- Zest and juice of 2 lemons
- 1/2 cup grated Parmigiano-Reggiano cheese
- Fresh parsley, chopped, for garnish
- Salt and pepper to taste

Instructions:

1. **Cook the Pasta:**
    - Boil linguine in salted water until al dente. Reserve some pasta water, then drain.
2. **Prepare the Sauce:**
    - In a skillet, heat olive oil and add lemon zest and juice. Cook for a minute to combine flavors.
3. **Combine:**
    - Toss the cooked linguine in the skillet, adding reserved pasta water for desired consistency. Stir in cheese, salt, and pepper.
4. **Serve:**
    - Serve hot, garnished with fresh parsley.

Farfalle alla Crema di Gorgonzola

Ingredients:

- 12 oz farfalle pasta
- 1 cup Gorgonzola cheese, crumbled
- 1 cup heavy cream
- 1/4 cup walnuts, chopped
- 2 cloves garlic, minced
- 1/4 cup olive oil
- Salt and pepper to taste
- Fresh parsley, for garnish

Instructions:

1. **Cook the Pasta:**
    - Boil farfalle in salted water until al dente. Reserve some pasta water, then drain.
2. **Prepare the Sauce:**
    - In a skillet, heat olive oil and sauté garlic until fragrant. Add heavy cream and Gorgonzola, stirring until the cheese melts.
3. **Combine:**
    - Toss the cooked pasta in the sauce, adding reserved pasta water for desired consistency. Stir in walnuts, salt, and pepper.
4. **Serve:**
    - Serve hot, garnished with fresh parsley.

www.ingramcontent.com/pod-product-compliance
Lightning Source LLC
LaVergne TN
LVHW081329060526
838201LV00055B/2528